Sonnets of Faith

DONA WILDING HAWS
ILLUSTRATED BY DAN BURR

Ambassador International

GREENVILLE, SOUTH CAROLINA & BELFAST, NORTHERN IRELAND

www.ambassador-international.com

Sonnets of Faith

© 2015 by Dona Wilding Haws
All rights reserved
Illustrated by Dan Burr

ISBN: 978-1-62020-522-8
eISBN: 978-1-62020-429-0

Scripture taken from The King James Version.

Cover Design and Page Layout by Hannah Nichols
eBook Conversion by Anna Riebe Raats

AMBASSADOR INTERNATIONAL
Emerald House
427 Wade Hampton Blvd.
Greenville, SC 29609, USA
www.ambassador-international.com

AMBASSADOR BOOKS
The Mount
2 Woodstock Link
Belfast, BT6 8DD, Northern Ireland, UK
www.ambassadormedia.co.uk

The colophon is a trademark of Ambassador

Printed in China

As a token of gratitude to my Savior, the
Lord Jesus Christ. May these lines ever
serve His purposes.

Let your light so shine before men, that they
may see your good works, and glorify your
Father which is in heaven.

—Matthew 5:16

Contents

Praise and Thanksgiving

Faith and Hope in Christ

Grace

Love

Peace and Rest

Prayer and Supplication

Character

Wisdom

Obedience

Ponderings

Welcome

Whether you nibble or feast, these verses were written for your delight. Perhaps you have not connected the gospel and poetry, yet everyone who has listened to or sung a hymn has experienced the gospel in poetic form. The sonnet, a specific form of poetry, uses imagery and word play to invite contemplation.

The sonnets in this book are written in the Shakespearean style. Each sonnet has fourteen lines divided into three groups of four lines, the quatrains, and two final lines making a couplet. Within each quatrain the last word of the first line rhymes with the last word of the third line and the last word of the second line rhymes with the last word of the fourth line. The three quatrains are followed by the couplet in which the ending words rhyme with each other.

All of the lines have ten syllables written in iambic pentameter, that is, a rhythm of five two-beat stresses, with a light-heavy feel, often described as duh-DUM duh-DUM duh-DUM duh-DUM duh-DUM.

Reading the reference Scripture first, opens the curtains, sets the stage, and turns on the footlights, illuminating to the mind the imagery and rhythm of the sonnets in vivid dimension. Brief notes following the reference Scriptures define uncommon words, archaic word forms, or give other helpful information.

Thank you for sharing the beauties of the gospel of Jesus Christ in *Sonnets of Faith*.

—Dona Wilding Haws

Praise and Thanksgiving

Jesus said unto her, I am the resurrection, and the life:
he that believeth in me, though he were dead, yet shall
he live:

—John 11:25

laud: praise

zephyrs: breezes

wane: weakening, atrophy

solace: comfort

balm: soothing crème

The Resurrection and the Life

Give thanks for sight and sound and scent today,

For eyes and ears and nose, declare Him laud,

For fragrant flow'rs that dip their heads and sway

On zephyrs sweet perfumed, thanks be to God.

But what of days when blossoms fresh have dried,

Their brittle petals strewn because of wane?

Whence comes the solace for sad eyes that cried?

Whence comes relief and healing balm for pain?

Be not afraid, He'll aid and comfort you,

He'll life and hope and light to you restore.

His promise of eternal life is true,

Supreme is He, our Savior evermore.

He has the pow'r o're sin, o're death, o're strife

He is the resurrection and the life.

O come, let us sing unto the Lord: let us make a joyful noise to the rock of our salvation. Let us come before his presence with thanksgiving, and make a joyful noise unto him with psalms.

—Psalm 95:1-2

descried: discovered, revealed

Come Make a Joyful Noise

Tell how express this music in my soul

So sweetly sings the harmony divine,

Resplendent chords for gifts Thou dost bestow,

A symphony from bount'ous love descried.

When Thou art near my self reverberates,

The strains sublime affording deepest peace

Crescendo in my heart to thus create

Sweet rhapsodies celestial without cease.

Come make a joyful noise unto the Lord

And sing a composition for His Grace;

A psalm of praise, for we shall be restored

To worship Him and kneel before His face.

The rock of our salvation here we praise

Exquisite are Thy high and holy ways.

And she brought forth her firstborn son, and wrapped him in swaddling clothes, and laid him in a manger; because there was no room for them in the inn . . . And, lo, the angel of the Lord came upon them, and the glory of the Lord shone round about them: and they were sore afraid. And the angel said unto them, Fear not: for, behold, I bring you good tidings of great joy, which shall be to all people. For unto you is born this day in the city of David a Saviour, which is Christ the Lord.

—Luke 2:7, 9-11

Now when Jesus was born in Bethlehem of Judaea in the days of Herod the king, behold, there came wise men from the east to Jerusalem, Saying, Where is he that is born King of the Jews? for we have seen his star in the east, and are come to worship him.

—Matthew 2:1-2

And it was about the sixth hour, and there was a darkness over all the earth until the ninth hour. And the sun was darkened, and the veil of the temple was rent in the midst. And when Jesus had cried with a loud voice, he said, Father, into thy hands I commend my spirit: and having said thus, he gave up the ghost.

—Luke 23:44-46

refulgence: brilliance, majesty

Everlasting Light

Shall I compare Thee with the sun so bright—
Warm radiance sent from the throne of God
That overcomes the darkness with pure light,
Refulgence grand creation doth afford.
Though in a stable low You laid Your head,
The heav'nly hosts proclaimed supreme design
And bright new star from East the wise men led
To worship, praise, adore Thee Lord divine.
Then when on Calv'ry's cross clouds hid the sun
And heaven wept with grief beyond compare,
In anguish precious blood did freely run,
A token of Thy cleansing pow'r declared.
Far brighter than in noonday's glow You live
And everlasting life and light You give.

I remember the days of old; I meditate on all thy works;
I muse on the work of thy hands. I stretch forth my
hands unto thee: my soul thirsteth after thee, as a thirsty
land. Selah.

—Psalm 143:5-6

verdure: greenery, freshness

I Will Trust

Shall I compare myself to thirsty earth,
Dust-sheathed and parched, in need of healing rain,
Sore shriveled, sunken spot of useless turf
Unfit for mowing, measured by disdain?
No, 'tis not so, for I can green anew
As plot refined by spring's fresh verdure grow
When gentle rains from Thee its strength renew,
So in me too a rescue Thou wilt sow.
The sun, the moon, the stars Thou didst create
And made this globe to share their orbits high;
Assigned Thou humankind to earth's estate,
With loving ardency their needs supply.
Lord God of heav'n and earth and sea and sky
Forever I will trust in Thee most High.

But if we walk in the light, as he is in the light, we have fellowship one with another, and the blood of Jesus Christ his Son cleanseth us from all sin.

—1 John 1:7

O Wondrous Gift

A gift when wrapped cannot be full enjoyed
'Til opened, comprehended, well received,
Inspected, studied, thoroughly employed,
Intelligence first grasped and then believed.
Administered, unfolded to our view
The love of Christ, His perfect charity
Will sanctify our souls to live anew,
Mend broken hearts and opens eyes to see—
To see most precious gifts e'er to be found
Of light and love and fellowship with God,
Full cleansed by holy sacrifice profound
We kneel in adoration, ever awed.
With souls pure washed the wondrous gift is giv'n
To lift by love and light each soul to heav'n.

And he is the propitiation for our sins: and not for ours only, but also for the sins of the whole world. And hereby we do know that we know him, if we keep his commandments.

—1 John 2:2-3

propitiation: atonement

solace: comfort, peace

Propitiation's Price

Redeemer mine who walked on earth and sea
'Cross gale-tormented waves and mountain's crest,
Of pearls in heav'n and earth You hold the key
Unlocking to my soul eternal rest.
Thy works sublime reveal a sacred treas're,
Example pure when followed I safe live;
And pondering Thy word brings keenest pleas're,
Blessed solace, strength, and courage will me give.
Though keeper of the jewels by royal birth,
Thy stewardship required full sacrifice
To sanctify God's children born on earth
Endowing us with everlasting life.
Propitiation's price by love full paid,
Transcendent sacrifice, for all have strayed.

And the Jews' Passover was at hand, and Jesus went up to Jerusalem, And found in the temple those that sold oxen and sheep and doves, and the changers of money sitting: And when he had made a scourge of small cords, he drove them all out of the temple, and the sheep, and the oxen; and poured out the changers' money, and overthrew the tables; And said unto them that sold doves, Take these things hence; make not my Father's house an house of merchandise. And his disciples remembered that it was written, The zeal of thine house hath eaten me up. Then answered the Jews and said unto him, What sign shewest thou unto us, seeing that thou doest these things? Jesus answered and said unto them, Destroy this temple, and in three days I will raise it up. Then said the Jews, Forty and six years was this temple in building, and wilt thou rear it up in three days? But he spake of the temple of his body. When therefore he was risen from the dead, his disciples remembered that he had said this unto them; and they believed the scripture, and the word which Jesus had said.

—John 2:13-22

endows: gives, grants

The Temple of His Body

When Jesus walked, He taught both high and humble

With ears to hear and hearts to understand

That temples built of man with ease may crumble,

But His high work was greater than of man.

From temple courts He drove out beasts and men,

Then from the Lord, the Jews would have a sign.

Destroy this temple answered He to them

And I will raise it up in three days' time.

The temple of His body He did give,

A sinless sacrifice for humankind,

Supreme His sacred work that we may live—

Give thanks with all your heart and soul and mind.

His vict'ry over death and o'er the grave

Endows eternal life—O wond'rous praise.

Faith and Hope in Christ

Then cometh he to a city of Samaria, which is called Sychar, near to the parcel of ground that Jacob gave to his son Joseph. Now Jacob's well was there. Jesus therefore, being wearied with his journey, sat thus on the well: and it was about the sixth hour. There cometh a woman of Samaria to draw water: Jesus saith unto her, Give me to drink . . . Then saith the woman of Samaria unto him, How is it that thou, being a Jew, askest drink of me, which am a woman of Samaria? for the Jews have no dealings with the Samaritans. Jesus answered and said unto her, If thou knewest the gift of God, and who it is that saith to thee, Give me to drink; thou wouldest have asked of him, and he would have given thee living water . . . Jesus answered and said unto her, Whosoever drinketh of this water shall thirst again: But whosoever drinketh of the water that I shall give him shall never thirst; but the water that I shall give him shall be in him a well of water springing up into everlasting life. The woman saith unto him, Sir, give me this water, that I thirst not, neither come hither to draw . . . The woman saith unto him, I know that Messias cometh, which is called Christ: when he is come, he will tell us all things. Jesus saith unto her, I that speak unto thee am he . . . And many more believed because of his own word; And said unto the woman, Now we believe, not because of thy saying: for we have heard him ourselves, and know that this is indeed the Christ, the Saviour of the world.

—John 4:5-7, 9-10, 13-15, 25-26, 41-42

Living Water

At Jacob's well the woman was amazed,
When Christ told her all she had ever done,
And quickly through the town the story blazed,
The hope of living water from the Son.
Confused was she and wondered what to think,
Yet when she understood she made request,
Dear Lord, from this pure water let me drink
Most surely it will ne'er leave me athirst.
Now as we read the Scripture, we review
Assurance to the woman at the well
And still the offer stands for me and you,
Those precious words of life the truth do tell.
Come drink from me and never thirst again—
You can be cleansed, washed free from ev'ry sin.

And God said, Let there be light: and there was light . . .
And God said, Let there be a firmament in the midst of
the waters, and let it divide the waters from the waters
. . . And God called the firmament Heaven. And the
evening and the morning were the second day. And
God said, Let the waters under the heaven be gathered
together unto one place, and let the dry land appear: and
it was so. And God called the dry land Earth; and the
gathering together of waters called he Seas: and God saw
that it was good . . . And God said, Let there be lights in
the firmament of the heaven to divide the day from the
night; and let them be for signs, and for seasons, and for
days, and years: . . . And God made two great lights; the
greater light to rule the day, and the lesser light to rule
the night: he made the stars also.

—Genesis 1:3, 6, 8-10, 14, 16

For God so loved the world, that he gave his only begotten
Son, that whosoever believeth in him should not perish,
but have everlasting life.

—John 3:16

omnipotence: God's power

enkindled: ignited, illuminated

God's Gifts

When God above declared, "Let there be light,"

And gave His token of celestial beam,

Omnipotence made plain to earthy sight

By masterpiece of love we've freely seen.

For planet, sea, and sky we here rejoice,

For sun and stars and moon's resplendent glow

Tell how can man with pen or tongue give voice,

For charities on us He doth bestow.

But if we do not recognize within

A rev'rence for this granted legacy

Then may enkindled sight in us begin

From glint to gleam enlarge that we may see—

Most excellent and greatest gift of all

Beloved Son, who saved us from the fall.

And she brought forth her firstborn son, and wrapped him in swaddling clothes, and laid him in a manger; because there was no room for them in the inn. And there were in the same country shepherds abiding in the field, keeping watch over their flock by night. And, lo, the angel of the Lord came upon them, and the glory of the Lord shone round about them: and they were sore afraid. And the angel said unto them, Fear not: for, behold, I bring you good tidings of great joy, which shall be to all people. For unto you is born this day in the city of David a Saviour, which is Christ the Lord. And this shall be a sign unto you; Ye shall find the babe wrapped in swaddling clothes, lying in a manger. And suddenly there was with the angel a multitude of the heavenly host praising God, and saying, Glory to God in the highest, and on earth peace, good will toward men. And it came to pass, as the angels were gone away from them into heaven, the shepherds said one to another, Let us now go even to Bethlehem, and see this thing which is come to pass, which the Lord hath made known unto us. And they came with haste, and found Mary, and Joseph, and the babe lying in a manger.

—Luke 2:7-16

Son of God

By night, a quiet watch the shepherds kept
Not knowing sacred scenes they sure would see
Angelic hosts proclaiming heav'n's elect
Our Lord and Savior, holder of the key.
Supreme and holy key to light and life
Sweet love of God now in a manger lay
With pow'r endowed to vanquish sin and strife
Unlocking to each soul salvation's sway.
The glory of the Lord shown round about
"Fear not," the angel said, oh sweet decree
Then with the tidings, they were freed from doubt
And said to one another, "Let us see—"
The precious key to victory o'er the grave
Dear Son of God, sent down our souls to save.

Now faith is the substance of things hoped for, the evidence
of things not seen.

—Hebrews 11:1

pellucid: clear, unblurred

natatorium: swimming pool

Things Not Seen

Where is the evidence of things not seen;
When not full seen, how shall this truth be found?
Pellucid faith we hold in high esteem
And faith in God doth all our woes confound.
Our voyage across life's vast and watered space
Imparts to sight an iceberg's frosty peak;
If we could see the whole through eyes of grace,
We'd see revealed the substance that we seek.
So swim the natatorium of life
Persistent, steady, staunch though billows roll
And find sheer strength beyond your pow'r to strive,
Sweet evidence of things seen through the soul.
Explore the heights of hope and trust in God,
Receive the gift of faith in Christ your Lord.

Wherefore seeing we also are compassed about with so great a cloud of witnesses, let us lay aside every weight, and the sin which doth so easily beset us, and let us run with patience the race that is set before us, Looking unto Jesus the author and finisher of our faith; who for the joy that was set before him endured the cross, despising the shame, and is set down at the right hand of the throne of God.

—Hebrews 12:1-2

rife: abundant

With Patience Win the Race

Consider now, does patience close compare

With baby steps a little child will take

To chase bright butterflies on breezes rare—

So 'cross the yard a journey she would make.

Then off she goes with step and thump and bump,

A nosedive in the grass does not deter;

There's more to life than sitting like a lump,

She's up and off, a tumble won't stop her.

Alert to learn and grow, with chances rife,

She'll try again and try 'til she can run

A patient winning race through her whole life,

She'll keep on going 'til the vict'ry's won.

You're not alone, with Him your problems face,

Have courage friend—with patience win the race.

Search the scriptures; for in them ye think ye have eternal life: and they are they which testify of me.

—John 5:39

erelong: before long

scrutinize: examine closely

denigrate: belittle

Witness

What? Look ye hither, thither, to and fro?
The testimony which ye seek is here,
But when 'tis spoken true ye say, "Not so,"
With hearts of stone, devoid of ears that hear.
Examine, scrutinize the written scroll,
Transform your hearts to more than paperweights.
That manuscript will edify your soul—
Prophetic witness do not denigrate.
Yes, trust the Scriptures and the words of John
For they will point you back again to Me.
Blessed with a broken heart you will erelong
Have hearing ears and tutored eyes that see.
I witness true that I am God's own Son,
Messiah, Royal King, the Holy One.

Grace

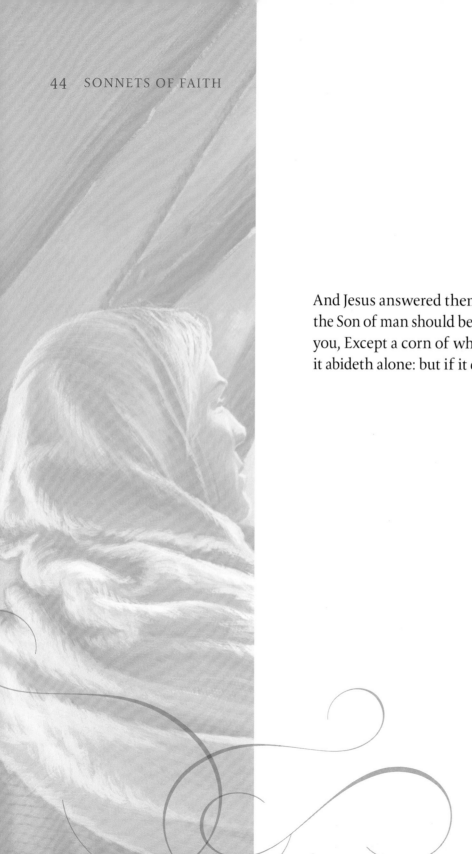

And Jesus answered them, saying, The hour is come, that the Son of man should be glorified. Verily, verily, I say unto you, Except a corn of wheat fall into the ground and die, it abideth alone: but if it die, it bringeth forth much fruit.

—John 12:23-24

Most Holy Fruit

Himself He did compare to corn of wheat

And said if it would die, it fruit could give.

Alone was He to measure full the feat

Required to cleanse our souls that we may live.

He knew at Calvary upon the cross,

Except this grain of wheat fall to the ground

It would not by its yield restore the loss

Of ev'ry human soul the world around.

His body from the tree laid in the tomb,

Then on the third day He in truth did rise

Thus from His work eternal life did bloom,

Transcendent gift of life above all prized.

Pure sacrifice He of himself did make,

Most holy fruit, we joyous do partake.

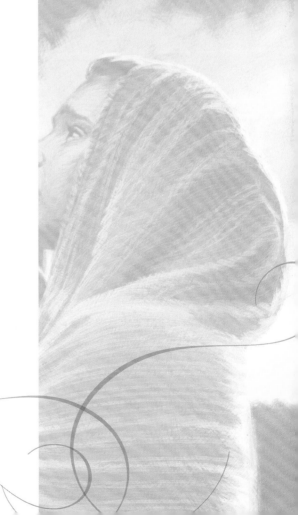

The grace of our Lord Jesus Christ be with you all. Amen.

—Romans 16:24

endow: give large gift

For Gifts of Grace

Of vast abundance come from Thee on High
And cherished through my heart's most inner core
Are thy great gifts of flow'rs and earth and sky
Enriching life, fresh fragrance I adore.
This subtle essence sweet around me stays
Imparting quiet strength to ev'ry task,
Confirming thy dear presence through my days,
A witness of thy grace in which I bask.
Bright daisies, roses, lilies of the field,
Providing nourishment for bird and bee,
Resplendent symbols of thy love, thy shield
To bring me in thy grace safe home to Thee.
With gratitude my Lord I humbly bow
For gifts of grace Thou dost to me endow.

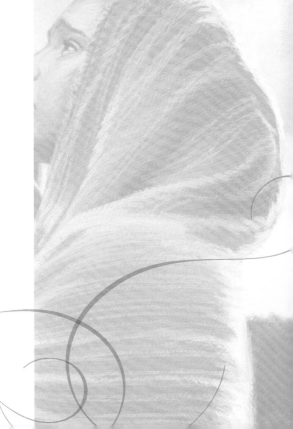

Jesus answered and said unto them, This is the work of God, that ye believe on him whom he hath sent. They said therefore unto him, What sign shewest thou then, that we may see, and believe thee? what dost thou work? Our fathers did eat manna in the desert; as it is written, He gave them bread from heaven to eat. Then Jesus said unto them, Verily, verily, I say unto you, Moses gave you not that bread from heaven; but my Father giveth you the true bread from heaven. For the bread of God is he which cometh down from heaven, and giveth life unto the world. Then said they unto him, Lord, evermore give us this bread. And Jesus said unto them, I am the bread of life: he that cometh to me shall never hunger; and he that believeth on me shall never thirst.

—John 6:29-35

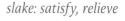

slake: satisfy, relieve

Heaven's Bread

A desert baker God did not require

The thousand's gone from Pharaoh's land to feed,

Yet manna's miracle would not inspire

Belief in God's own Son, by slav'ry's seed.

Now God will have us take of food divine,

To chew, digest, incorporate into

A soul well nourished wherein we combine

Warm bread of life in all we say and do.

Christ is the bread of life come down from heav'n,

The nurture sent from God for all to sup.

Gaunt hunger slake by banquet freely giv'n

With Christ's pure sustenance be lifted up.

Supreme the sacred fare He does outpour,

Come feast on heaven's bread forevermore.

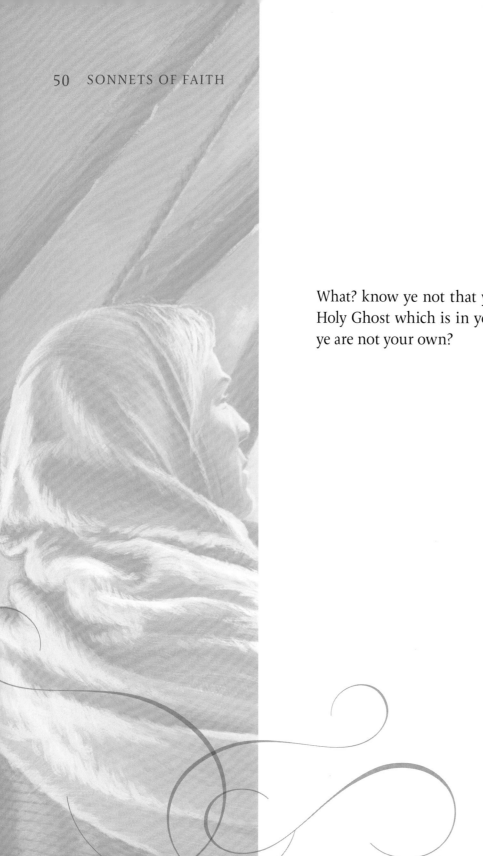

What? know ye not that your body is the temple of the Holy Ghost which is in you, which ye have of God, and ye are not your own?

—1 Corinthians 6:19

The Holy Ghost

How shall I see the Holy Ghost in me?

My person, temple giv'n for His abode,

A legacy from God to help me see

His love for me through hallowed gift bestowed.

This sacred gift, most beautiful and rare

Gives comfort, wisdom, knowledge beyond price.

Name, if you can, a treasure to compare

To grace this living temple free of vice.

Conclude you then this exercise in thought

Acknowledging sound proof of heaven's will

With dawning through the Holy Ghost when sought,

The sacred truth from God He doth instill.

Within my temple walls this light divine

Illuminates my soul with grace sublime.

Howbeit when he, the Spirit of truth, is come, he will guide you into all truth: for he shall not speak of himself; but whatsoever he shall hear, that shall he speak: and he will shew you things to come.

—John 16:13

bedim: darken

Sacred Writ: Holy Scriptures

bequest: gift

The Spirit of Truth

Who is this guide of whom the Savior spoke,
Who witness bears and testifies of Him
And with assurance fans the flame of hope,
An inner glow when outward lamps bedim.
For John in Sacred Writ set down the plan,
A faithful scroll recording this bequest
Of witness for the Christ giv'n unto man,
A glowing testimony for the blessed.
Then what if that bright beam should flicker dim
With banished hope by battles sorely fought?
The promise stands confirmed, we can know Him,
Through flame rekindled when 'tis truly sought.
He'll guide you to all truth, show things to come—
Reveal to you the Father and the Son.

Those things, which ye have both learned, and received, and heard, and seen in me, do: and the God of peace shall be with you.

—Philippians 4:9

scrutiny: close examination

Sacred Writ: Holy Scriptures

infusing: inspiring, implanting

The Tutor

Come talk of peace and charity my friend,
Most cherished is your company and loved.
Reward my time that I may comprehend,
Through scrutiny see gifts from God above.
When we converse I offer no debate,
For in thy precepts pure will strength be giv'n
To open to my view and elevate
The pow'rs of grace divine that lead to heav'n.
Then what of days when peace is not enjoyed
And I conduct myself as ne'er befits
A follower of Christ who has employed
The friend who tutors me—the Sacred Writ.
Thy lessons read, received and now are mine
Infusing precious hope and peace sublime.

If I do not the works of my Father, believe me not. But if I do, though ye believe not me, believe the works: that ye may know, and believe, that the Father *is* in me, and I in him.

—John 10:37-38

Work of the Heart

My life on earth comprises much of work,
Foremost of which is beating of my heart.
My lifeblood's pump sustains me, does not shirk
For when it does, then shall my life depart.
Remember Christ, His valiant work most pure,
Without His sacred work I cannot live,
By caring grace He does my life assure
Immortal gratitude to Him I'll give.
His work flows through me now and without cease,
Eternal source of sanctity and light;
And when I leave this earth in sweet release
At one with Him I'll dwell, O blessed delight.
Because His life-force beats anew in me
I shall with Christ and Father ever be.

Love

Neither do men light a candle, and put it under a bushel, but on a candlestick; and it giveth light unto all that are in the house. Let your light so shine before men, that they may see your good works, and glorify your Father which is in heaven.

—Matthew 5:15-16

scanty: little, meager

Let Your Light Shine

When dusk draws nigh, I do a candle light
So all within the house have means to see.
Then I remember Christ's eternal sight
And ponder His injunction unto me.
Said Christ, come let your light shine before all
Reflecting greatest glory to your God.
Dear Father, help me carry out this call
Well knowing I am not a little flawed.
The Light of Life my scanty spark ignites
And with His blaze I shall grow brighter still.
Oh help me Lord, a flame of faith excite,
An inner strength to carry out Thy will.
I'll let my light shine bright, as bright as can be
And pray that those who see will honor Thee.

Charity suffereth long, and is kind; charity envieth not; charity vaunteth not itself, is not puffed up, Doth not behave itself unseemly, seeketh not her own, is not easily provoked, thinketh no evil; Rejoiceth not in iniquity, but rejoiceth in the truth; Beareth all things, believeth all things, hopeth all things, endureth all things.

—1 Corinthians 13:4-7

bestowal: gift, grant

Charity

Come ponder precious treasure, dear to buy,
The price of which requires no evil soul;
Not envy, nor starched pride can e'er supply
The key engaging charity's bestowal.
Tell who will suffer long and still be kind,
Is not puffed up and seeketh not their own
But seeketh for the good of humankind,
Rejoicing in the truth wherever sown.
Kind charity believeth in all things—
All things which edify from God above,
Employ of which to humble heart doth bring
The key to Christ's most pure and holy love.
Blessed charity will teach us how to live
And open to us treasures Christ will give.

And this commandment have we from Him, That he who loveth God love his brother also.

—1 John 4:21

tutelage: teaching

benevolent: kind

Know This Commandment

Know this commandment come from God above

And demonstrated by our Savior true,

A tutelage that teaches us to love

With courses for our schooling not a few.

Benevolent and wise, our Father saw

That children of necessity be taught;

Tuition's cost for His refining law

By patient daily practice to be bought.

True love of God perfects the earthy soul

From kindergarten to a Ph.D.

Compassion grown from God's exalted goal—

Curriculum divine for you and me.

For love of God and Christ refines the heart

'Til we to every soul Their love impart.

I wait for the Lord, my soul doth wait, and in his word do
I hope. My soul waiteth for the Lord more than they that
watch for the morning: I say, more than they that watch
for the morning.

—Psalm 130:5-6

sate: filled, satisfied

deterging: cleanse, purify

That Holy Dawn

A brill'ant summer morn of rosy glow
Illuminates my soul with love for Thee.
Its splendid rays the darkness overthrow,
Celestial beams now lighting hope in me.
Then on my knees I bend in fervent prayer
Renewing praise for bounties from Thy Child,
Redemption's work to free us from all snare,
My Savior's work of love and mercy mild.
I wait and watch for days to come when I
Receive Thy presence 'til I am full sate.
On cleansing pow'r from Him I do rely,
Deterging from corruption's low estate.
As others watch for morn, I'll watch for Thee
And on that holy dawn shall wait on Thee.

Judas saith unto him, not Iscariot, Lord how is it that thou wilt manifest thyself unto us, and not unto the world? Jesus answered and said unto him, If a man love me he will keep my words; and my Father will love him, and we will come unto him, and make our abode with him.

—John 14:22-23

codex: earliest form of books

tome: large, heavy or learned book

The Blessed Books

Be scroll or codex, paperback will do,

Clear essence of His word must sure be kept;

Then will both Christ and Father come to you,

Abide in love and always you protect.

A simple task with so refined an end,

To listen and to do with loving heart.

With good news from our Lord we will transcend

The taint and wounds of Satan's wild-flung dart.

So from His book receive the words of life

And in your book show steadfast love for Him,

Then when your tome is closed to toil and strife

Receive of God's pure presence—love full brim.

May love of Christ and Father 'bide with you,

Be manifest in all you say and do.

A new commandment, I give unto you, That ye love one another; as I have loved you, that ye also love one another.

—John 13:34

And he arose, and rebuked the wind, and said unto the sea, Peace, be still. And the wind ceased, and there was a great calm.

—Mark 4:39

And Jesus said, Make the men sit down, Now there was much grass in the place. So the men sat down, in number about five thousand. And Jesus took the loaves; and when he had given thanks, he distributed to the disciples, and the disciples to them that were set down; and likewise of the fishes as much as they would. When they were filled, he said unto his disciples, Gather up the fragments that remain, that nothing be lost. Therefore they gathered them together, and filled twelve baskets with the fragments of the five barley loaves, which remained over and above unto them that had eaten.

—John 6:10-13

And when he thus had spoken, he cried with a loud voice, Lazarus, come forth. And he that was dead came forth, bound hand and foot with graveclothes: and his face was bound with a napkin. Jesus saith unto them, Loose him, and let him go.

—John 11:43-44

This New Commandment

A new commandment give I unto you
That you will follow Me—yes ev'ry day,
In thought and word and deed, disciple true
Bold manifest in what you do and say.
Remember Lazarus who now does live,
Commandment to the winds and waves, "Be still,"
And sup to thousands, with My thanks, did give,
In all I've carried out My Father's will.
This new commandment give I unto you,
To serve with love as you did see in Me
And I will magnify the works you do
Through gifts divine, clear evidenced in thee.
This new commandment give I unto you
And charge you now, love one another true.

Peace and Rest

Are not two sparrows sold for a farthing? and one of them shall not fall on the ground without your Father. But the very hairs of your head are all numbered. Fear ye not therefore, ye are of more value than many sparrows.

—Matthew 10:29-31

Sparrow's Fall

See thou the stars in heav'n of royal birth
By that celestial being over all,
He made the vast expanse above the earth
And yet takes note of tiny sparrow's fall.
Of His creations high we are most blessed,
Protected, loved, and guided by His hand,
Though ills of life may fill us with unrest
And sorrows wrench our souls with full command.
Then, if we do not trust His holy care
To lead us on our journey here below,
With blank and hollow eye afore we stare
Oblivious to loving help bestowed.
Trust God who knows of ev'ry sparrow's fall—
Beloved child, you are most blessed of all.

Peace I leave with you, my peace I give unto you: not as the world giveth, give I unto you. Let not your heart be troubled, neither let it be afraid.

—John 14:27

discernment: understanding

banishes: removes

My Peace I Give to You

When darksome clouds cast shadows o'er my life

And wretched is my soul—I cry to God,

Please can there not be more than toil and strife?

Pray help me Father trust Thy Holy Word.

Discernment of the print upon the page,

Unfolds Thy precious pledge assuring me,

Let not your heart be troubled or afraid—

So draws the somber veil that I may see.

The promise of Thy word brings dawning light,

A beaming now reveals an inner peace

And banishes bleak clouds beyond my sight,

All torments flee my heart in hushed release.

Now come dear child, your confidence renew,

Be not afraid—My peace I give to you.

And when they had sent away the multitude, they took him even as he was in the ship. And there were also with him other little ships. And there arose a great storm of wind, and the waves beat into the ship, so that it was now full. And he was in the hinder part of the ship, asleep on a pillow: and they awake him, and say unto him, Master, carest thou not that we perish? And he arose, and rebuked the wind, and said unto the sea, Peace, be still. And the wind ceased, and there was a great calm. And he said unto them, Why are ye so fearful? how is it that ye have no faith? And they feared exceedingly, and said one to another, What manner of man is this, that even the wind and the sea obey him?

—Mark 4:36-41

Note: The Sea of Galilee has several names including: Harp Lake, Lake of Gennesaret, or Lake Tiberias.

abaft: to the rear

fraught: full of

sodden: soaked, drenched

Peace Be Still

Abaft of ship lay Jesus safe asleep

While Harp Lake's flood did quake afore the blast,

Destruction hovered o're the angry deep,

Huge waves and wretched rushed the shiv'ring mast.

Each raucous blow with deadly peril fraught,

The sodden men rushed aft with anguished cries,

Dear Master—save us that we perish not.

Then spoke the Lord of life and sea and skies.

Becalmed were winds and waters and the soul,

For thus spake He with mild and gentle voice,

The Lord and Savior in His noble role

Commanded peace—now let us too rejoice.

Redeemer, Lord Messiah in whose will

We trust now and forever—Peace be still.

Thou wilt keep him in perfect peace, whose mind is stayed
on thee: because he trusteth in thee.

—Isaiah 26:3

stayed: abide, continue

Perfect Peace

Praise God whose gracious gifts are without cease
To those whose thoughts are stayed upon the Lord,
For He will keep them in His perfect peace,
A promise sure, found in His Holy Word.
The gift of peace, most precious and rare found
Is giv'n to those who think on Deity.
Tell who is there be high or low renown,
Has learned there to reside and been set free.
Set free from torments of a troubled mind,
Set free by trust in God who knows the end
Of sorrows small and great, and how to find
The perfect peace we seek, our souls to mend.
This claim to perfect peace is not ignored
By those whose minds are stayed upon the Lord.

The effectual fervent prayer of the righteous man availeth much.

—James 5:16b

endowment: large gift

supplication: prayer

bequest: gift

The Dove of Peace

How shall I know the peace of God's great love?

Tranquility, assurance most divine

Descending o're my soul from realms above,

Endowment of His gentle grace, now mine.

Now mine because the gift is freely giv'n,

My supplication granted on request,

Transcendent Dove of Peace come down from heav'n,

Announcing and affirming His bequest.

But if the dove of peace flees from my heart,

Then shall I kneel to God in fervent prayer

And beg Him once again, I pray impart

Serenity most valuable and rare.

As James affirmed in times now long-since past,

Gifts can be had when we sincere will ask.

Then shall the kingdom of heaven be likened unto ten virgins, which took their lamps, and went forth to meet the bridegroom. And five of them were wise, and five were foolish. They that were foolish took their lamps, and took no oil with them: But the wise took oil in their vessels with their lamps. While the bridegroom tarried, they all slumbered and slept. And at midnight there was a cry made, Behold, the bridegroom cometh; go ye out to meet him. Then all those virgins arose, and trimmed their lamps. And the foolish said unto the wise, Give us of your oil; for our lamps are gone out. But the wise answered, saying Not so; lest there be not enough for us and you: but go ye rather to them that sell, and buy for yourselves. And while they went to buy, the bridegroom came; and they that were ready went in with him to the marriage: and the door was shut. Afterward came also the other virgins, saying, Lord, Lord, open to us. But he answered and said, Verily I say unto you, I know you not. Watch therefore, for ye know neither the day nor the hour wherein the Son of man cometh.

—Matthew 25:1-13

stayed: abide, continue

endowed: graced, supplied

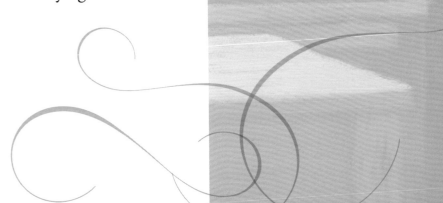

My Lamp

'Twas Jesus taught that preparations made

Devoted, resolute, would fill our lamps

With fuel of faith to hold us fully stayed

On Christ our Lord, endowed by holy amps.

Then drop by drop we build our fuel supply

Both in our lamp and outward vessel full,

Till ev'ry veil of darkness we defy

With wick well trimmed, by Christ made whitest wool.

Thence for the Bridegroom I will watch and pray,

A fervent prayer that I with Him abide

In perfect harmony ne'er more to stray,

My little flame in Him vast multiplied.

Redeemer, King, and Savior of my soul,

Far brighter than the sun at noonday's glow.

And the very God of peace sanctify you wholly; and I pray
God your whole spirit and soul and body be preserved
blameless unto the coming of our Lord Jesus Christ.

—I Thessalonians 5:23

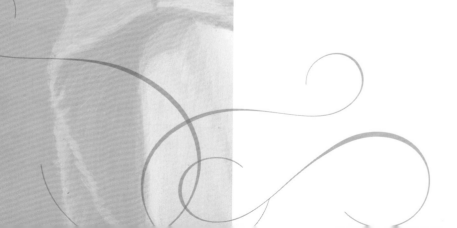

reminisce: go over in one's memory

munificence: generosity, goodness

sanguine: cheerful, optimistic

My Prayer

Come hear my sonnet for a human friend—
With views of light and love from heav'n above,
Assurance from the Lord your soul to lend,
A reminisce of God's eternal love.
To rhyme and then to verse this prayer is set,
A humble lyric brim with earnest praise
For God whose kind munificence begets
The hope of life and joy beyond the grave.
Now friend—if you refuse to hear my words,
As if on deafened ears they chance to fall,
I'll sanguine be for Father God has heard
My uttered prayer for you and for us all.
Please may His gracious goodness now impart
A healing pow'r to sanctify our hearts.

And Moses took the rod from before the Lord, as he commanded him. And Moses and Aaron gathered the congregation together before the rock, and he said unto them, Hear now, ye rebels; must we fetch you water out of this rock? And Moses lifted up his hand, and with his rod he smote the rock twice: and the water came out abundantly, and the congregation drank, and their beasts also.

—Numbers 20:9-11

marbled: like marble, as in hardness or coldness

quarried: cut from rough stone and refined

My Quarried Heart

Whence come compliant heart and contrite soul,
The willingness to hear and then to do,
A laundered self, not grimy like to coal,
A purity fresh born in me anew?
When Moses with God's pow'r did strike a rock
He brought forth saving water's blessed flow,
So from my marbled heart can God unlock
A spring of faith in Christ from me to grow.
Pure living waters from the Christ ne'er cease,
Thirst-quenching, life-restoring, cleansing through—
Eternal sacred fount of holy peace,
O make my quarried heart forever true,
Obedient and stalwart, unafraid,
My life, my soul on Thee forever stayed.

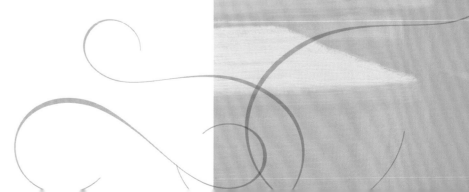

Being born again, not of corruptible seed, but of incorruptible, by the word of God, which liveth and abideth for ever . . . But the word of the Lord endureth for ever. And this is the word which by the gospel is preached unto you.

—I Peter 1:23, 25

Sacred Writ: Holy Scriptures

corruptible: may be or become unclean, polluted

Seeds of Change

How can I change corruptible for not—

For I am weak, to this I surely own.

With God's illumination truly sought

I search for seeds of change to soon be sown.

But how this sowing make? What form to take?

What stock from Sacred Writ will help me grow

'Til thoughts of fresh delights begin to make

A garden nourished by His heav'nly glow?

Abundant nurture shown me hour by hour,

Vitality from God has granted root;

From seed to stem to leaf and on to flow'r

'Til by His love I taste of ripened fruit.

O Thou who plantest seeds of change in me—

May I abide in Thee, eternally.

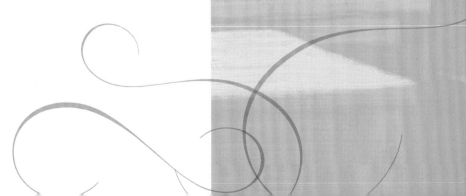

Behold, I stand at the door, and knock: if any man hear my voice, and open the door, I will come in to him, and will sup with him, and he with me.

—Revelations 3:20

laud: praise, honor

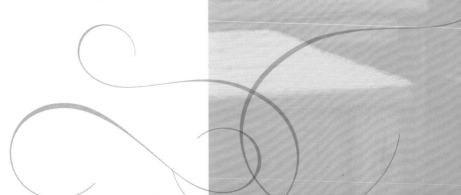

The Door

The Scriptures guide to ask, to seek, to knock
And thus it shall be opened unto you.
On whose side of the door is found the lock
Which opens wide inviting Him to school—
To school your heart, your mind, your ev'ry day.
And gently lead you safely home to God
With help from Him in all you do and say—
For this we ever thankful bring Him laud.
He taught that we must ask and seek and knock
With humble hearts prepared to learn of Him.
Now we control the key that turns the lock
To that most vital door which lets Him in.
Do ask and seek and knock your whole life through,
Throw open wide the door, He'll come to you.

Character

I can do all things through Christ which strengtheneth me.
—Philippians 4:13

succor: help, sustenance

staunch: resolute, steadfast

behest: command, precept

All Things Through Christ

So is the soul as fine physique in flesh,
A construct of exertion's staunch pursuit,
Refining work designed at God's behest,
By Grace assistance giv'n to institute.
Contract, elongate muscle, sinew too
For building strong anatomy robust.
Maturing of the soul will have its due
And with His help we can receive this trust.
Despite that feeble knees do not bear up
But tremble 'neath their burden's heavy load
With succor from the Savior freely sup
Receiving strength most gen'rously bestowed.
Through Christ we can lift ev'ry burden asked,
And with His pow'r be fit for every task.

Wherefore, holy brethren, partakers of the heavenly call-
ing, consider the Apostle and High Priest of our profession,
Christ Jesus; Who was faithful to him that appointed him,
as also Moses was faithful in all his house. For this man
was counted worthy of more glory than Moses, inasmuch
as he who hath builded the house hath more honour
than the house. For every house is builded by some man;
but he that built all things is God. And Moses verily was
faithful in all his house, as a servant, for a testimony of
those things which were to be spoken after; But Christ
as a son over his own house; whose house are we, if we
hold fast the confidence and the rejoicing of the hope
firm unto the end.

—Hebrews 3:1-6

espoused: employed

Divine Work

A house does not just happen, it is built
And when 'tis built does not the builder rule
Though safe, secure, and warm as Grandma's quilt,
It is a house and serves us as a tool.
Consider well the builder of the house
Comparing him to Christ our Lord and guide;
With study on construction tools espoused
We'll learn to build by tutoring supplied.
Then does the Christ build souls or kingdom first?
Or is it that the souls a kingdom make?
Creator, King, and Lord of universe,
Who gave Himself a ransom for our sake—
Divine His work that purifies from sod
A soul well made, prepared to dwell with God.

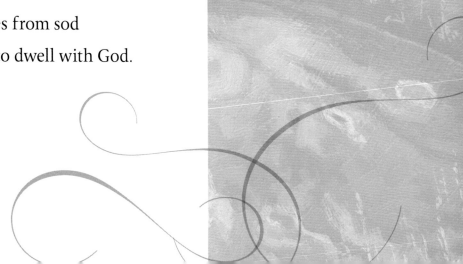

For if ye forgive men their trespasses, your heavenly Father will also forgive you: But if ye forgive not men their trespasses, neither will your Father forgive your trespasses.

—Matthew 6:14-15

deterged: cleansed

If Ye Forgive . . .

When I will make my body clean, I show'r
Removing ev'ry trace of soil and stink,
Renewed by cleansing water's earthly pow'r
Upon my inner self I start to think.
Now what of oily scum do I find there?
What smear or stain or grease spot do I see?
How does my core concealed with skin compare,
Is it deterged and rinsed of all debris?
Will Christ to me an inward wash supply,
A cleansing, healing solvent for my soul?
On His almighty aid I will rely;
His teachings pure in truth my heart console.
I thank Thee Lord, I'll follow Thy decree—
If ye forgive, ye shall forgiven be.

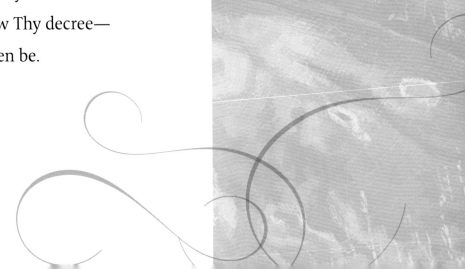

And Jesus sat over against the treasury, and beheld how the people cast money into the treasury: and many that were rich cast in much. And there came a certain poor widow, and she threw in two mites, which make a farthing. And he called unto him his disciples, and saith unto them, Verily I say unto you, That this poor widow hath cast more in, than all they which have cast into the treasury: For all they did cast in of their abundance; but she of her want did cast in all that she had, even all her living.

—Mark 12:41-44

scarcity: lack, shortage

guileless: free of deceit, in truth

More or Less

You've heard that more is less and less is more;
Example here is given when 'twas so,
Recorded in Mark's book in days of yore
By widow's hand, two mites she did bestow.
'Twas precious little, those two copper coins
Yet 'twas her treasure, all that she could give.
Her giving caused a scarcity to loins
Which filling helps the human body live.
Here less is more, as this dear lady knew—
So Christ revealed, esteeming her highborn,
Then taught His friends how in her virtue grew,
A heartfelt gift her withered hands adorned.
Our God delights to bless the human heart
When guileless, we to Him of self impart.

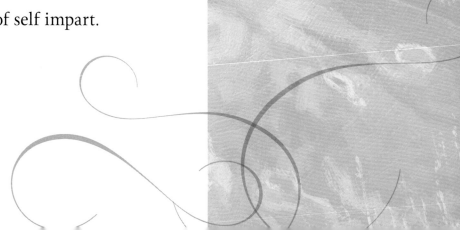

Judge not according to the appearance, but judge righteous judgment.

—John 7:24

tittle: bit, very small part

Righteous Judgment

'Tis thought that—that we see we think we know

And that we know, we think we see complete.

Investigation shows it is not so.

Example of this folly oft we meet.

A grov'ling worm we view and judge low-formed

Ne'er dreaming that this worm will one day fly,

On leaving swaddling bands becomes transformed

To be the stately Monarch of the sky.

Then to all humankind let us apply

The lesson that chaste nature clearly shows,

For judgment true we cannot safe rely

On tittle gleaned by eyes and ears and nose.

 A righteous judgment fair be ever sought—

 According to appearance judge ye not.

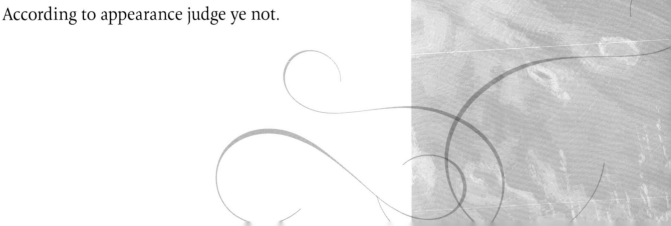

While the Pharisees were gathered together, Jesus asked them, Saying, What think ye of Christ? whose son is he? They say unto him, The Son of David. He saith unto them, How then doth David in spirit call him Lord, saying, The Lord said unto my Lord, Sit thou on my right hand, till I make thine enemies thy footstool? If David then call him Lord, how is he his son? And no man was able to answer him a word, neither durst any man from that day forth ask him any more questions.

—Matthew 22:41-46

What Think Ye of Christ?

Of questions posed in newspapers we read
A date, a time, a place, a motive sworn,
How? What? Who? Why? When? Where was done
the deed,
With evidence, a testimony born.
'Twas Jesus asked a group of Pharisees
Of whom and what and whence the Christ
would come,
And reasoned with the "hows" to help them seize
Their fallacy of thought to its full sum.
Now here we pose the question yet anew—
If printed in the news or in your heart
Tell what ye think of Christ, what is your view,
Will you a witness sure to all impart?
He is the resurrected Son of God,
Our Savior, Jesus Christ, oh bring Him laud.

Wisdom

Therefore whosoever heareth these sayings of mine, and doeth them, I will liken him unto a wise man, which built his house upon a rock: And the rain descended, and the floods came, and the winds blew, and beat upon that house; and it fell not: for it was founded upon a rock. And every one that heareth these sayings of mine, and doeth them not, shall be likened unto a foolish man, which built his house upon the sand: And the rain descended, and the floods came, and the winds blew, and beat upon that house; and it fell: and great was the fall of it.

—Matthew 7:24-27

A Home with God

A house well built on Christ's foundation stands,
With blueprint, walls, and roof of grand design,
Constructed strong to weather all demands
Each sojourn in mortality assigns.
Said Christ, of those who build upon My rock,
From storm and wind and flood you are secure,
For strength begat in heav'n does God unlock,
Protection born of God you will procure.
When Satan's dark destructions 'gainst you rage
Be wise my friend, do more than hearers do,
Be quick the pow'r of God to full engage,
Obeying Christ will hurricanes subdue.
We're building mansion's frame—not hut of sod,
With blueprint giv'n of Christ, for home with God.

The fear of the Lord is the beginning of wisdom: a good understanding have all they that do his commandments: his praise endureth for ever.

—Psalm 111:10

unfeigned: sincere, genuine

extol: praise, adore

Beginning of Wisdom

What is this rev'rence called the fear of God,
Which rev'rence proved deep permeates the soul,
With love unfeigned delights to bring Him laud
In thought, in word, in deed doth Him extol.
True wisdom's nub begins by rev'rence pure,
Rich understanding comes through word well kept
With evidence clear cut, discerned, secure,
Craved comprehension for which saints have wept.
For wisdom like a diadem when cut
And fashioned by the mighty master's hand
Reveals through facets sheared clear light, not blunt,
A brill'ance not before at our command.
In wisdom's strength comes rev'rence some call fear
Of God and Christ—intelligence most dear.

A new commandment I give unto you, That ye love one another; as I have loved you, that ye also love one another. By this shall all men know that ye are my disciples, if ye have love one to another.

—John 13:34-35

behest: command, precept

exhort: encourage, persuade

Love One Another

Most brilliant light had come on earth to dwell,

Our Lord, the Christ gave all to please His God,

Then to disciples loved He bid farewell

A flawless beam that lit the path ne'er trod.

Divine behest to His disciples true

Were thus recorded in the Book of John,

"Love one another as I have loved you,"

Betoken love by works as I have done.

How shall this ardent flame in me be lit—

Exhort my very soul with love to glow

That I become a valiant servant fit

To serve the master where'er I may go?

Essential this command I live and do—

Love one another as I have loved you!

Then said Jesus to those Jews which believed on him, If ye
continue in my word, then are ye my disciples indeed; And
ye shall know the truth, and the truth shall make you free.

—John 8:31-32

sooth: fact, reality

Truth

In John we read, "the truth shall make you free."

Then what is truth and where is truth, how found?

For truth is not clear shown in what you see

Nor safely evident in all surround,

Not transparent nor readily the sooth,

Revealed, uncovered to the human mind.

We ask, we seek, we knock in search of truth,

But where and when and how this gem to find?

The words of Christ will teach us what to do.

Abide in Christ, be valiant now, be bold,

Courageously the upward path pursue

Emboldened by His promises of old.

Esteemed and priceless jewel, this guarantee—

Come learn the truth and truth shall make you free.

He that saith, I know him, and keepeth not his commandments, is a liar, and the truth is not in him. But
whoso keepeth his word, in him verily is the love of God
perfected: hereby know we that we are in him. He that
saith he abideth in him ought himself also so to walk,
even as he walked.

—I John 2:4-6

vigil: watchful attention

stalwart: strong, valiant

Walk the Walk

Some people say you've got to walk the walk—
Now what walk have you got to walk, my friend?
And too they say, you've got to talk the talk,
But how to talk and where to walk depend
On what you want to say and where you'll go.
So walk and talk, but choose the reasons why.
With words and deeds, you vital seeds will sow
And seeds will harvest give in by and by.
Then why this talk and walk, my friend, what goal
Demands a constant vigil day and night?
Prime harvest grows from plantings in the soul
Robust with nourishment from Heav'nly light.
Be stalwart friend, the Savior's path pursue—
Reflect His light in all you say and do.

If any of you lack wisdom, let him ask of God, that giveth to all men liberally, and upbraideth not; and it shall be given him. But let him ask in faith, nothing wavering. For he that wavereth is like a wave of the sea driven with the wind and tossed.

—James 1:5-6

endowed: granted

bereft: lacking, missing

boon: advantage, benefit

Wisdom's Gift

Be you a seeker true of wisdom fair?

Come hear the words of James on this bequest—

By faith we may receive of gifts so rare

From God to us endowed on clear request.

Almighty God will grant us wisdom's gift

To be unwrapped and savored day by day

And by His kindness we'll nay be bereft

Of help and hope and guidance on our way.

But what if you have not the faith to ask—

How shall you then of wisdom's boon partake?

With James believe that God's great love is vast,

He in your breast a faithful heart can make.

Be wise enough to ask for faith to ask

For wisdom's noble strength in ev'ry task.

Obedience

Finally, brethren, whatsoever things are true, whatsoever things are honest, whatsoever things are just, whatsoever things are pure, whatsoever things are lovely, whatsoever things are of good report; if there be any virtue, and if there be any praise, think on these things.

—Philippians 4:8

rife: abundant, bountiful

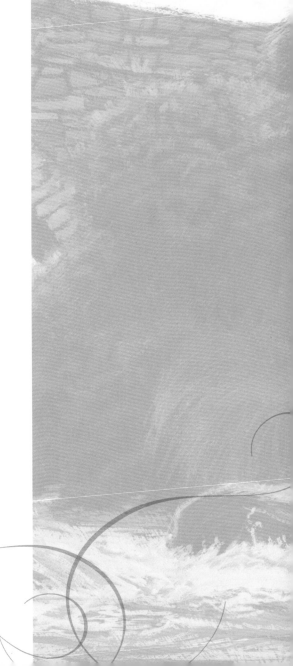

Cross the Footbridge

We think on things that bring us near to Christ
And in so thinking open to our view
A path less trod with scenes of glory rife
Requiring patient footsteps to pursue.
Now whatsoever things are true, we seek,
And whatsoever things are virtuous.
And whatsoever things are just, we seek,
And whatsoever things of good report.
And whatsoever things are lovely seek
And whatsoever things are pure, we seek.
And whatsoever things are honest seek
And whatsoever things are praiseworthy.
First seek in thought and then convert to deed,
To cross the footbridge making us Christ's seed.

For I have given you an example, that ye should do as I have done to you.

—John 13:15

fixity: determination

pristine: pure

Example Bright

By Jesus lustrous work in Galilee

He taught that we should do as He had done.

Examples excellent we humbly see

And pray, "Help me to emulate Thy Son."

Endowed by the almighty from above

He healed and taught and fed each one who asked.

He did His Father's work with purest love,

A sacred fixity blessed ev'ry task.

Pray radiance from His resplendent light

Illuminate my soul that I may see

My path to service with a heart that's right

To do the work that He assigns to me.

Of pristine blaze, there is no brighter found—

He lights the way that leads to higher ground.

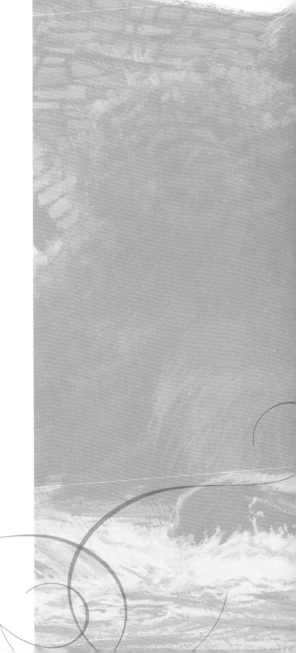

And he stretched forth his hand toward his disciples, and said, Behold my mother and my brethren! For whosoever shall do the will of my Father which is in heaven, the same is my brother, and sister, and mother.

—Matthew 12:49-50

Family with God

Now whosoever does the Father's will
Becomes a part of Christ's own family.
Consider here this doctrine to distill—
Then bind in fam'ly ties with Him to be.
Said He referring to disciples true,
My mother, brother, sister here reside
Together bound as Father's will we do,
For ye with me in Father's love abide.
Then why would some the choice of orphan make
Forsaking home and hearth and family?
Do they not see that Christ died for our sake
And by His tender mercy set us free?
Set free to be refined from lump of sod
Into a holy family with God.

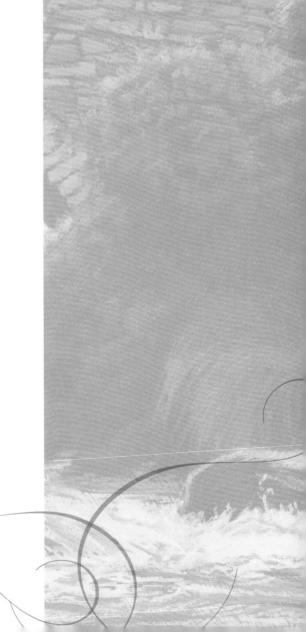

And in the sixth month the angel Gabriel was sent from God unto a city of Galilee, named Nazareth, To a virgin espoused to a man whose name was Joseph, of the house of David; and the virgin's name was Mary. And the angel came in unto her, and said, Hail, thou that art highly favoured, the Lord is with thee: blessed art thou among women. And when she saw him, she was troubled at his saying, and cast in her mind what manner of salutation this should be. And the angel said unto her, Fear not, Mary: for thou hast found favour with God. And, behold, thou shalt conceive in thy womb, and bring forth a son, and shalt call his name JESUS. He shall be great, and shall be called the Son of the Highest: and the Lord God shall give unto him the throne of his father David: And he shall reign over the house of Jacob for ever; and of his kingdom there shall be no end. Then said Mary unto the angel, How shall this be, seeing I know not a man? And the angel answered and said unto her, The Holy Ghost shall come upon thee, and the power of the Highest shall overshadow thee: therefore also that holy thing which shall be born of thee shall be called the Son of God. And, behold, thy cousin Elisabeth, she hath also conceived a son in her old age: and this is the sixth month with her, who was called barren. For with God nothing shall be impossible. And Mary said, Behold the handmaid of the Lord; be it unto me according to thy word. And the angel departed from her.

—Luke 1:26-38

Mary

Of gracious daughters, virtuous and fair
By God were you called here to intercede;
Extraordinary work of essence rare,
His servant pure to meet most sacred need.
From heav'n above sent God His angel true
Announcing favor with the Lord you'd found.
Alone of women He hath chosen you,
A call from Him, to bless the world full round.
When Gabriel gave voice you doubted not
And said, "Behold the handmaid of the Lord."
May trials endured with gravest sorrow fraught
Be consecrated to your high reward.
You filled your high commission mother mild,
Sweet Mary, Mother of the Holy Child.

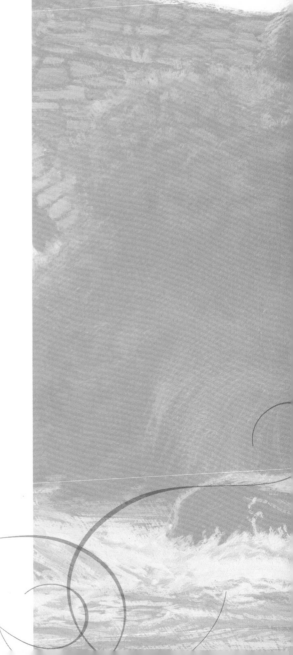

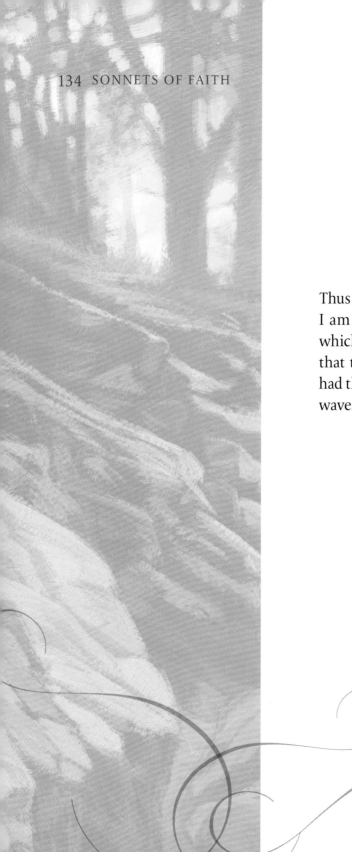

Thus saith the Lord, thy Redeemer, the Holy One of Israel;
I am the Lord thy God which teacheth thee to profit,
which leadeth thee by the way that thou shouldest go. O
that thou hadst hearkened to my commandments! then
had thy peace been as a river, and thy righteousness as the
waves of the sea:

—Isaiah 48:17-18

Peace as a River

I am the Lord thy God, Redeemer true,

The Holy One of Israel who will guide

With clear commandments given unto you

To lead through troubled straits, safe in Me 'bide.

O may thy peace be as a river's flow

Sustaining life, thirst quenching evermore,

A font of living water I'll bestow,

Receive celestial blessings from My store.

If thou, My child will hearken to My word,

Then can thy righteousness be like the sea

Whose waves' majestic pow'r I do afford

A promise from your loving Deity.

Commandments kept will strength in you renew,

I am the Lord thy God, Redeemer true.

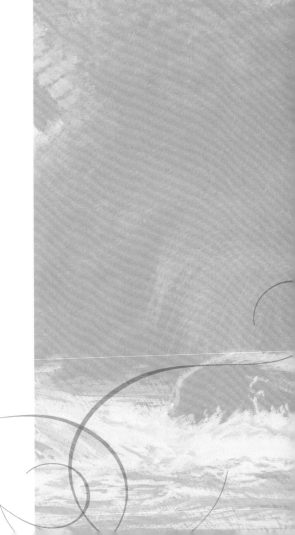

Thou shalt have no other gods before me.

—Exodus 20:3

eminence: prestige

The First Commandment

Some say that play and leisure must afford
A life athrill comprising all that's game.
Some say career and bankroll move toward
The pow'r and eminence composing fame.
Know that surprises come to one and all,
'Cause when so snuggly in their coffin placed
This is the question posed to great and small—
The majesty of God did you disgrace?
For Moses heard, "I am the Lord thy God,"
Then carried down the tablets made of stone
On which God's finger wrote His Holy Word
And to all people made His will well known.
I made the earth and more than eye can see—
Thou shalt no other gods have before me.

But when the Pharisees had heard that he had put the Sadducees to silence, they were gathered together. Then one of them, which was a lawyer, asked him a question, tempting him, and saying, Master, which is the great commandment in the law? Jesus said unto him, Thou shalt love the Lord thy God with all thy heart, and with all thy soul, and with all thy mind. This is the first and great commandment.

—Matthew 22:34-38

perfervid: impassioned

The Great Commandment

Perfervid Pharisee would tempt our Lord
Examining the law—how does it stand?
Then taught the Christ to him we must afford
Devotedness to God with full command.
A precept pure of light and love divine
To bring us safely home to God above,
Though o're life's gorge and crag we sure must climb
Ascending step by step on pow'r of love.
The great commandment said our Savior true
Is loving God with mind and soul and heart.
Fixed on this path He will reveal to you
His holy plan sublime in ev'ry part.
Through giving all our heart and mind and soul
We glorify our God and reach our goal.

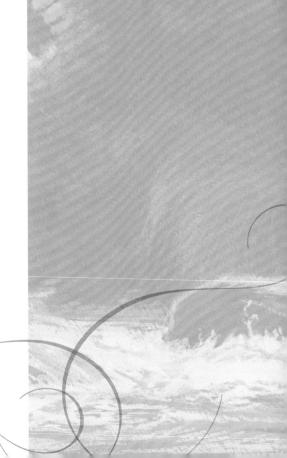

Ponderings

And when the Sabbath was past, Mary Magdalene, and Mary the mother of James, and Salome, had bought sweet spices, that they might come and anoint him . . . And entering into the sepulchre, they saw a young man sitting on the right side, clothed in a long white garment; and they were affrighted. And he saith unto them, Be not affrighted: Ye seek Jesus of Nazareth, which was crucified: he is risen; he is not here: behold the place where they laid him . . . Now when Jesus was risen early the first day of the week, he appeared first to Mary Magdalene, out of whom he had cast seven devils. And she went and told them that had been with him, as they mourned and wept. And they, when they had heard that he was alive, and had been seen of her, believed not. After that he appeared in another form unto two of them, as they walked, and went into the country. And they went and told it unto the residue: neither believed they them. Afterward he appeared unto the eleven as they sat at meat, and upbraided them with their unbelief and hardness of heart, because they believed not them which had seen him after he was risen.

—Mark 16:1, 5-6, 9-14

plumb: probe, explore

petrified: hardened

embodiment: framework, personification, anatomy

query: question, challenge

Within My Heart

By angel, Christ sent witness to the women
Then spake with Mary at the tomb's rolled door.
He walked the dusty road, new come from heaven
Confirming witness He had borne afore.

Disciples could not then the truth receive
Though Christ Himself had told them He would come.
Inviting those who would to pure believe,
The depths of crippled hearts He here did plumb.

Then what of hearts benumbed and petrified
Through incapacitating doubt and fear?
Will they stand blinded at the Savior's side,
Embodiment of truth will they revere?

Here begs the query I to self impart—
What sees the Master deep within my heart?

And again, departing from the coasts of Tyre and Sidon, he came unto the sea of Galilee, through the midst of the coast of Decapolis. And they bring unto him one that was deaf, and had an impediment in his speech; and they beseech him to put his hand upon him. And he took him aside from the multitude, and put his fingers into his ears, and he spit, and touched his tongue; And looking up to heaven, he sighed, and saith unto him, Ephphatha, that is, Be opened. And straightway his ears were opened, and the string of his tongue was loosed, and he spake plain.

—Mark 7:31-35

emending: mending, healing

Emending Touch

Now Christ was newly come to Galilee

With sacred works, His witness aft and 'fore,

Of healing sick and making blind to see

As never had been done on earth before.

No lapping of the waves was heard that day

By deaf-afflicted man who scarce could speak,

'Til with pure healing touch Christ did defray

Imprisonment's full chains born by the weak.

Inquiry comes which I to self exhort,

What malady in me waits Christ to heal,

What deafness of my soul will He deport,

What clear emending touch will He reveal?

For precious gift of mercy I rely

On Thee, Blessed Redeemer, Lord Most High.

And when it was evening, his disciples came to him, saying, This is a desert place, and the time is now past; send the multitude away, that they may go into the villages, and buy themselves victuals. But Jesus said unto them, They need not depart; give ye them to eat. And they say unto him, We have here but five loaves, and two fishes. He said, Bring them hither to me. And he commanded the multitude to sit down on the grass, and took the five loaves, and two fishes, and looking up to heaven, he blessed, and brake, and gave the loaves to his disciples, and the disciples to the multitude. And they did all eat, and were filled: and they took up of the fragments that remained twelve baskets full. And they that had eaten were about five thousand men, beside women and children.

—Matthew 14:15-21

When the people therefore saw that Jesus was not there, neither his disciples, they also took shipping, and came to Capernaum, seeking for Jesus. And when they had found him on the other side of the sea, they said unto him, Rabbi, when camest thou hither? Jesus answered them and said, Verily, verily, I say unto you, Ye seek me, not because ye saw the miracles, but because ye did eat of the loaves, and were filled . . . And Jesus said unto them, I am the bread of life: he that cometh to me shall never hunger; and he that believeth on me shall never thirst.

—John 6:24-26, 35

unfeigned: sincere, genuine

Daily Bread

In days of old five thousand men were fed,
And women too and children also supped.
Twelve basketsful remained of barley bread,
The fragments His disciples gathered up.
And though all ate the fishes and the bread
First light knew hunger's empty pinch unfeigned.
Did they remember what the Savior said?
Within their souls did words of life remain?
Some hungers can't be fed with fork and knife,
Sweet nourishment doth come from Christ our Lord.
Receive said He, I am the Bread of Life,
Refreshment pure to you I will afford.
Our bodies and our souls will be restored
By feasting from the bounties of the Lord.

And straightway Jesus constrained his disciples to get into the ship, and to go before him unto the other side, while he sent the multitudes away. And when he had sent the multitudes away, he went up into a mountain apart to pray: and when the evening was come, he was there alone. But the ship was now in the midst of the sea, tossed with waves: for the wind was contrary. And in the fourth watch of the night Jesus went unto them, walking on the sea. And when the disciples saw him walking on the sea, they were troubled, saying, It is a spirit; and they cried out for fear. But straightway Jesus spake unto them, saying, Be of good cheer; it is I; be not afraid. And Peter answered him and said, Lord, if it be thou, bid me come unto thee on the water. And he said, Come. And when Peter was come down out of the ship, he walked on the water, to go to Jesus. But when he saw the wind boisterous, he was afraid; and beginning to sink, he cried, saying, Lord, save me. And immediately Jesus stretched forth his hand, and caught him, and said unto him, O thou of little faith, wherefore didst thou doubt? And when they were come into the ship, the wind ceased. Then they that were in the ship came and worshipped him, saying, Of a truth thou art the Son of God.

—Matthew 14:22-33

Simon Bar Jonah

From Simon Bar Jonah we learn to trust
And gain by his examples strong and weak—
Disciples of the Lord will soon adjust
And try and try again, for strengths we seek.
On sea one night the Savior chose to walk,
And Simon begged, may I come unto Thee?
Because of faltered faith we do not mock,
Though Simon's faith did briefly from Him flee.
When frenzied waves of life the soul rough rock,
On Simon think—let not your heart be ill,
For Christ our Lord did on the water walk
And faith in Christ bids troubled hearts be still.
Have faith in Christ our Lord full ev'ry hour,
For He will lift us up with saving pow'r.

And there are also many other things which Jesus did, the which, if they should be written every one, I suppose that even the world itself could not contain the books that should be written. Amen.

—John 21:25

pix: picture

writ: archaic form for written

The Library

Shall we compare the earth so well supplied
With evidence of gracious work divine,
And testimony Scriptures true confide
As God's great work all people to refine—
Shall we compare all these with libraries
Full housed with ev'ry kind of well-shelved book,
Recorded files of sun and sky and seas,
Of realms of thought and pix on which to look?
For John did say, if all Christ did were writ,
Abundance of His works we do not know,
Said sacred record likely would not fit
Upon His footstool where we dwell below.
And as John said, so we can sure believe,
As proof from sun and stars we still receive.

Alphabetical Index

Scripture Index

Dona Wilding Haws has taught Sunday School and led Gospel Discussion Groups for adults and children in various congregations for over 30 years. She has a Degree in Psychology. She is a creative cook, believes in the power of giving and receiving forgiveness, and delights in seeing beauty in all of God's creations.

www.donawildinghaws.com

donawildinghaws@gmail.com

More work by Dan Burr can be seen at www.danburr.com.

For more information about
AMBASSADOR INTERNATIONAL
please visit:

www.ambassador-international.com
@AmbassadorIntl
www.facebook.com/AmbassadorIntl

"Deep searching thoughts, of Scripture born, filled me with *faith*, and *hope* reborn. Dona Wilding Haws' precious gift, born of *charity*, edifies and enlightens the soul, reveals the light and love of Christ, and invites prayerful meditation. Once inside its pages I could not cease to explore, for true joy is truly at its core."

—K. Newell Dayley
Composer and Lyricist

"Kindred spirits will find many rewards in these pages."

—Richard Bushman
Gouverneur Morris Professor of History Emeritus
Columbia University

"In this beautiful little book, Dona Wilding Haws has shown us how to turn a testimony into art. It's a process we all should try."

—Claudia L. Bushman

Sonnets of Faith is destined to be a favorite "go to" for inspiration and comfort for those who love the Lord and those who want to feel His love. Cherished Bible passages from the King James Version set the stage as you witness the Scriptures come to life in a new dimension through the lyrics and rhythms of sonnets. The vivid and specially-commissioned work, of award-winning artist Dan Burr, resonates with the sonnets, adding his full-color vision to this unique collection. Whether you spend a few minutes or a few hours, you'll come away enriched, guided, and more secure in the Lord's unfailing love for you.

Ambassador International
GREENVILLE, SOUTH CAROLINA & BELFAST, NORTHERN IRELAND
www.ambassador-international.com

U.S. $25.99/U.K. £18.99

ISBN 978-1-62020-522-8

9 781620 205228

52599

EAN